You're a Business Owner,
NOT A DUMMY!

You're a Business Owner, NOT A DUMMY!

Understand Your Merchant Account

MICHAEL MINTZ

iUniverse, Inc.
Bloomington

You're a Business Owner, Not a Dummy!
Understand Your Merchant Account

iUniverse books may be ordered through booksellers or by contacting:

iUniverse
1663 Liberty Drive
Bloomington, IN 47403
www.iuniverse.com
1-800-Authors (1-800-288-4677)

ISBN: 978-1-4759-2224-0 (sc)
ISBN: 978-1-4759-2223-3 (hc)
ISBN: 978-1-4759-2222-6 (e)

Library of Congress Control Number: 2012907811

Printed in the United States of America

iUniverse rev. date: 10/16/2012

Dedicated to my wife, Meredith, and my two sons, Ben and Alex. Their love and endless support inspire me every day.

Contents

Introduction

If you are reading this book, unfortunately you are not one of the lucky few to have a cash-only business. In order to compete in today's global marketplace, it is essential that businesses large and small accept credit and debit cards from their customers. Credit and debit card usage continues to increase. If you don't want your customers going to your competitors, you must accept plastic.

There is so much that can be said about the merchant processing industry. Many books have been written on the topic, but most of them exceed two hundred pages and are more like textbooks. This is not meant to be a textbook, but instead is more of a reference guide for business owners and financial executives.

In the United States, in order for any business to accept credit and debit cards, a merchant account needs to be set up. There are plenty of service providers out there offering merchant processing services, but how can a business owner or financial executive decide which of the many salespeople are telling the truth and which ones are only looking to maximize their own profit on the deal?

Merchant accounts are offered by a variety of entities, including local, regional, and national banking institutions; direct processors/ acquirers; and a vast network of independent sales organizations (ISOs). If you are already accepting credit and debit cards, you probably receive multiple solicitations every month for these services.

As it stands, here is the situation:

- You want to get the best deal for your organization, but there is so much to understand.

- The market is filled with "low rates" and "great deals" offered by various merchant services providers.

- In order to make the right decision, you need to fully understand how merchant processing works.

If only there were a simple one-stop resource to get all the knowledge you need to make the right decision.

Well, now there is.

Obtaining a merchant account is not difficult. Understanding your merchant account and the crazy world of credit card processing is not as simple. Forget trying to understand your month-end statement. That practically requires a PhD.

Having run a successful merchant services business, I have heard all of the customer complaints and the many horror stories of how business owners have been taken advantage of by their merchant services providers. That is exactly why I decided to write this book.

It is time for business owners to be in the know and fully understand how their merchant accounts work.

The wide breadth of topics and easy-to-understand structure of this guide make it a must-read for all business owners and financial executives responsible for merchant account decisions.

Take the time to understand how it all works. You will not be disappointed.

I promise to clear the air and provide you with the full working knowledge necessary to make the right merchant services provider decision for your organization.

How This Book Is Organized

This book is broken up into nine chapters, each covering a topic related to merchant processing. The goal is for anyone who reads this book to be in the know the next time a merchant services provider salesperson knocks on the door.

The content in each chapter stands alone, so you don't have to read all the chapters in order. Take a look through the table of contents to find a single topic of interest, or read the entire book to gain a complete understanding.

CHAPTER 1
How Does the Credit and Debit Card Process Work?

This chapter will discuss

- key industry terms;
- the different ways merchants accept credit and debit card payments;
- who all the players are; and
- the step-by-step electronic payment process.

The first step to understanding the world of merchant processing is to become more familiar with the industry lingo.

Key Industry Terms

ABA Routing Number

The American Banking Association (ABA) routing number is a unique, bank-identifying number that directs electronic ACH deposits to the proper bank. The number consists of nine digits and precedes the account number printed at the bottom of a check.

Acquiring Bank or Acquirer

The banking institution that provides its clients with the ability to accept electronic forms of payment. An acquiring bank teams with a processor to set up a merchant account for a client.

Address Verification Service (AVS)

A service that verifies the cardholder's billing address. Utilizing an AVS is applicable to certain types of businesses (mail order, telephone order, or Internet-based) in order to help combat fraud in card-not-present transactions.

Adjustment

When a correction to a transaction is required, this is handled by making an adjustment.

American Express

A financial organization that issues credit cards and acquires transactions, unlike Visa and MasterCard, which are bank associations.

Annual Fee

A fee charged by some merchant services providers on an annual basis. Annual fees are sometimes referred to as membership fees.

Application Fee

A one-time fee charged by merchant services providers that covers the cost of merchant account underwriting, approval, and setup.

Approval

The process by which a transaction is approved by an issuing bank. Approvals are requested via an authorization, which ensures the cardholder has the appropriate credit limit or bank account balance to honor his or her financial obligation.

Assessments

Assessments are the portion of interchange fees charged by Visa, MasterCard, and Discover. As of October 1, 2011, assessments are 0.11 percent for Visa and MasterCard and 0.10 percent for Discover, calculated on the dollar amount of the transaction.

Authorization

An authorization is a request made by the merchant to charge a cardholder. The authorization must be settled (see batch settlement) in order to charge the actual credit or debit account. If batch settlement does not occur within a specified time frame, the charge will drop off and not be funded; the customer will not be charged; and the merchant will not be paid.

Authorization Code

The numeric or alphanumeric code provided by the issuing bank that references the transaction for internal and external reporting purposes.

Authorization Response

The response provided by the issuing bank to the acquiring bank and ultimately to the merchant when an authorization is initiated. Responses include approval, decline, and referral.

Automated Clearing House (ACH)

The automated clearing house network is a nationwide, wholesale electronic payment and collection system. It is a method of transferring funds between banks via the Federal Reserve System.

Automatic Bill Payment

An agreement between a merchant and a cardholder allowing recurring, periodic billing using a credit or debit card for goods or services rendered (for example, when a patient goes to the dentist and promises to pay off his $1,200 bill in twelve equal $100 installments that will occur on the first day of each month for twelve months). This is also called recurring billing.

Average Ticket (Average Transaction Amount)

The average dollar amount of a merchant's credit and debit card transactions calculated by dividing the total dollar volume of monthly transactions by the total number of monthly transactions.

Basis Point

A basis point is equal to one one-hundredth of a percentage point. Discount rates are expressed in basis points.

1 Basis Point = 0.01% and 100 Basis Points = 1.00%

Batch

A collection of transactions submitted for settlement. It is good business practice to run a batch once a day.

Batch Settlement

The process by which a merchant submits all transactions that occur throughout the day to its acquiring bank for settlement and deposit into its business bank account.

Capture

The process of capturing funds from an authorization. The acquiring bank captures funds from the issuing bank on behalf of its client (the merchant).

Card Associations

A network of issuing banks and acquiring banks that process payment cards of a specific brand. Familiar payment card association brands include Visa, MasterCard, and Discover.

Card-Not-Present (CNP) Transactions

When the cardholder and the card are not physically present at the time the transaction occurs. Typical card-not-present transactions take place in industries focused on business-to-business, mail order, telephone order, and Internet-based transactions.

Card-Present Transactions

When the cardholder and the card are physically present at the time the transaction occurs. Card-present transactions account for the majority of credit and debit card transactions in the world. Also called swiped transactions.

Card Verification Value Code (CVV)

The card verification value code is used to help authenticate a customer's credit or debit card in card-not-present transactions. For Visa (CVV2) and MasterCard (CVC2), the code will be the last three digits printed on the back of the card. For American Express (CID), the code will be the four-digit number on the front of the card above the account number.

Chargeback

The process by which funds that have been paid to a merchant are taken back because of a disputed or improper transaction. A chargeback is typically initiated by the consumer/cardholder. Merchants are often assessed a fee for each chargeback regardless of the ultimate outcome.

Commercial, Corporate, or Business Cards

Credit or charge cards issued by businesses to cover expenses for their employees such as travel and entertainment.

Credit

The nullification of a prior authorized and settled transaction where funds are returned to the customer.

Debit Card

A bank card used to purchase goods and services and to obtain cash. When a debit card is used, the cardholder's personal bank account is debited for the amount of the purchase. Certain debit card transactions require a personal identification number (PIN) for use. Debit cards branded with a bank card logo (Visa or MasterCard) can be accepted without a PIN.

Decline

A transaction that is not approved by the issuing bank. A decline by an issuing bank means the bank will not authorize the request made by the acquiring bank because of either a lack of funds or lack of credit on the cardholder's account.

Discount Rate

A percentage rate-based fee. The discount rate is multiplied by the dollar amount of each transaction to calculate the discount fee owed. Discount rates are applicable to both interchange fees and the fee to the acquirer, processor, ISO, or bank.

Discover

Discover Financial Services is a direct banking and payment services company. Discover operates the Discover Network, their credit card payments network; the PULSE network ("PULSE"), their automated teller machine ("ATM"), debit and electronic funds transfer network; and Diners Club International, their global payments network. ("2010 Form 10-K, Discover Financial Services". United States Securities and Exchange Commission. http://www.sec.gov/Archives/edgar/data/1393612/000119312511014919/d10k.htm.)

Downgrade Fee

An additional fee charged to a merchant for mid-qualified and nonqualified transactions. Downgrade fees are typical in fixed-rate pricing when a low rate is promised to the merchant but the actual all-in rate is much higher to accept certain types of credit and debit cards (for example, rewards cards or corporate cards).

Independent Sales Organization (ISO)

A company that independently solicits potential merchants on behalf of an acquirer or a processor.

Interchange

The process by which all banking parties involved in a credit or debit card transaction (processors, acquirers, issuers) manage the processing, clearing, and settlement of credit and debit card transactions, including the assessment, collection, and distribution of fees between parties.

Interchange Fee

A fee paid by an acquiring bank to an issuing bank for transactions entered into interchange. The interchange fee consists of a discount rate applied to the dollar amount of each transaction as well as a transaction fee (swipe fee).

A transaction must meet certain predetermined criteria to be categorized in a specific interchange category. Each transaction is evaluated individually, so it is possible for each monthly transaction a merchant processes to have a different interchange fee associated with it.

Interchange fees are ultimately passed along to the merchant.

Internet Merchant Account

A specific type of merchant account that is required for merchants who wish to sell goods and services over the Internet and accept credit and debit cards as payment via a company website. Transactions that occur on this type of an account are considered card-not-present transactions and require a payment gateway.

Issuing Bank or Issuer

Any banking institution that offers credit and debit cards to its clients. Virtually all banking institutions in the United States are issuing banks.

7

Keyed-In Transaction

A transaction that involves keying in the credit or debit card account number using a computer or standalone credit card terminal. Keyed-in transactions occur in card-not-present environments such as mail order, telephone order and Internet-based businesses.

Manual Close

A batch settlement that is manually initiated by the merchant on a daily basis.

MasterCard

A leading global payments company that provides a critical economic link among financial institutions, businesses, merchants, cardholders and governments worldwide, enabling them to use electronic forms of payment instead of cash and checks. ("2010 Form 10-K, MasterCard Incorporated". United States Securities and Exchange Commission. http://www.sec.gov/Archives/edgar/data/1141391/000119312511044721/d10k.htm.)

Merchant

A retailer or any other entity that agrees to accept credit and/or debit cards from its customers.

Merchant Account

A commercial account that enables a merchant to accept credit cards, debit cards, and other forms of electronic payment.

Merchant Agreement

A written agreement between a merchant and an acquiring bank/processor containing their respective rights, duties, and obligations with respect to acceptance of credit cards, debit cards, and other forms of electronic payment as well as matters related to bank card activity associated with the merchant account.

Merchant Identification Number (MID)

A unique number that is assigned by the acquirer/processor to identify a merchant and maintain proper financial records.

Merchant Services Provider (MSP)

An entity that provides merchant services to business owners. Merchant services providers consist of acquirers, processors, ISOs, and banks.

Throughout this book MSP will be used interchangeably with acquirers, processors, ISOs, and banks.

Monthly Statement

The communication from the MSP to the merchant detailing the credit and debit card transactions that occurred in a specific month and the associated fees.

MO/TO

Mail order/telephone order.

Nonqualified

A broad industry term that describes a transaction that holds a higher percentage of risk to the issuing bank.

Transactions are categorized as nonqualified for various reasons, including

- the manual entry of credit or debit card information,
- failure to settle the transaction in a timely manner, or
- the type of credit or debit card presented to the merchant.

Examples of nonqualified cards include rewards, international, and corporate cards.

Payment Gateway

A computer-based system that facilitates the processing of credit and debit card transactions over the Internet. Payment gateways will encrypt sensitive information to ensure a secure transmission between the parties involved.

PCI DSS (Payment Card Industry Data Security Standard)

A worldwide information security standard assembled by the founding payment brands of the Payment Card Industry Security Standards Council (PCI SSC), including American Express, Discover Financial Services, JCB International, MasterCard Worldwide, and Visa Inc. International. The PCI DSS is a set of comprehensive requirements designed to help organizations proactively protect customer account data.

Point of Sale (POS)

A location where credit and debit card transactions are performed with the cardholder present. POS terminals facilitate transactions.

Processor

A large data center that processes credit and debit card transactions in addition to settling merchant funds utilizing an acquiring bank relationship. A processor connects to the merchant on behalf of an acquiring bank via a standalone terminal, payment gateway, or POS system to process payments electronically.

Reserve

A reserve or holdback is established by the issuing bank to help alleviate risk associated with higher-volume and higher-risk merchants. Reserves may be funded by a merchant with a cash deposit or a percentage of gross sales.

Retrieval Request

A request initiated by a cardholder or issuing bank for documentation concerning a transaction. A retrieval request can lead to a chargeback.

Secure Sockets Layer (SSL)

An encryption system that allows merchants to process transactions securely over the Internet.

SIC Code

Standard industry classification code. Four-digit number used to identify a specific business type.

Swiped Transaction

A transaction that involves credit or debit card information being transferred directly to the processor as a result of swiping or sliding the card through a card reader or POS terminal. Also called a card-present transaction.

Transaction Fee

A fee charged to a merchant for each credit or debit card transaction. Transaction fees are in addition to any discount rate. Transaction fees are a part of interchange fees and can also be a part of the additional fees charged by an MSP.

Visa

A global payments technology company that connects consumers, businesses, banks and governments in more than 200 countries and territories, enabling them to use digital currency instead of cash and checks. ("2010 Form 10-K, Visa Inc.". United States Securities and Exchange Commission. http://www.sec.gov/Archives/edgar/data/1403161/000119312510265236/d10k.htm)

Voice Authorization

An authorization that is obtained over the phone. If the transaction is approved, the merchant is provided with an authorization code, which is used to settle the transaction through a credit card terminal, POS terminal, or payment gateway at a later time. There are often additional fees associated with a voice authorization.

Void

The reversal of an approved transaction that has been authorized but not settled. In order to reverse settled transactions, a credit must be processed.

Different Ways Merchants Accept Credit and Debit Card Payments

The majority of credit and debit card transactions are sent electronically to acquiring banks and issuing banks for authorization, capture, and settlement. Various methods exist for presenting a credit or debit card sale to the payments system. In all circumstances, one of the following things occur:

- the entire magnetic strip on the back of the card is read by a swipe through a credit card terminal or POS terminal;
- a computer chip is read; or
- credit or debit card information is manually entered into a credit card terminal, computer, or website.

A credit card terminal

- is a standalone piece of electronic equipment that allows a merchant to input transaction information and swipe or key-enter credit or debit card information;
- is typically plugged into a power supply and connected to a telephone line or an Internet-based (IP) connection; and
- may be powered by batteries and communicate through a cellular phone data network.

When a credit or debit card is processed (either swiped or keyed-in), the credit card terminal contacts the various networks via the acquirer/processor for authorization.

An automated response unit or ARU is also known as a voice authorization, capture, and deposit.

- An ARU allows for manual keyed-in entry (no swipe) and authorization of a credit or debit card over a cellular or land-line telephone.

- A merchant imprints a customer's card with an imprinter to create a customer receipt and merchant copy and then processes the transaction over the phone.

A payment gateway is a computer-based system that facilitates the processing of transactions over the Internet. Payment gateways encrypt sensitive information to ensure that information passes securely between the parties involved.

- The acquiring bank/processor will typically be a separate company from the payment gateway provider.

- Some MSPs have their own proprietary payment gateways.

- The majority of companies use third-party payment gateway providers.

The payment gateway usually has two components:

1. A virtual terminal that allows a merchant to securely log in and key in credit and debit card numbers; and

2. A website shopping cart that connects to the payment gateway via an API connection to allow for real-time processing from the merchant's website.

Business Cards

Visa and MasterCard have created a specialized type of credit card used primarily by government agencies and larger businesses. Increasingly, corporations and government agencies are relying on this form of payment to compensate their service providers and suppliers. Businesses benefit by receiving their funds quickly and by winning competitive bids and government contracts where purchasing cards are the required form of payment. The downside, however, is the increased cost associated with receiving these payments.

B2B Electronic Solutions

Corporations across the United States are taking advantage of a wide array of new innovative electronic payment solutions. Paper check payment on accounts payable is slowly moving to an ACH-based payment method and more advanced card association-based solutions that can extend a company's days payable outstanding (DPO) as well as provide financial incentive from a wide variety of issuing banks. Companies such as *Boost Payment Solutions* are pioneering new innovative solutions with corporate America and federal, state, and local governments. The card associations and other third party vendors are providing unique services that provide both payer and vendor efficiencies and benefits.

Level 2 and Level 3 Data

Large corporations may qualify for ways to process transactions that allow them to pay lower fees if they can supply additional information, called level 2 or level 3 data. For example, if government transactions are over $5,000, businesses can significantly reduce their transaction costs by including level 2 or level 3 data about the purchase along with each transaction. Examples of level 2 or level 3 data include the purchase order number associated with the transaction that the credit card will be paying. This data is passed on by the purchaser so that it is easier to reconcile the transaction.

Who Are the Players?

An *issuing bank* markets various financial services to its customers, including credit and debit cards. Banking customers have a wide variety of choices to fit their specific business needs, including debit, credit, rewards, and corporate cards.

Most people are aware that issuing banks will apply an interest rate to purchases and cash advances when their clients do not pay their credit card bills in full at the end of each month. What many people are not aware of is that the same issuing bank makes a percentage (discount rate) and a transaction fee from each purchase their customers make using their bank-issued credit or debit cards. These discount rates and transaction fees are set by the card associations and vary depending on the type of card (debit, credit, rewards, or corporate).

An *acquiring bank* teaming with a *processor* establishes the merchant account for the business owner (merchant) and is responsible for transmitting customer credit and debit card information to the issuing bank for approval and ultimate collection of funds on behalf of the merchant.

An independent sales organization (*ISO*) is a company that independently solicits potential merchants on behalf of an acquirer/processor.

- ISOs come in many sizes from single-person operations to large multi-office organizations.
- ISOs can represent one or many acquirers/processors offering clients various industry solutions.
- ISOs have a specific "buy rate" or cost of goods from the acquirer/processor, which is usually stated as a cost over interchange (fees).
- The ISO decides how to mark up its cost of goods to the merchant. The amount the ISO receives over and above their buy rate is profit to the ISO.
- Examples of ISOs are AMG Payment Solutions, North American Bankcard, Pay Simple, and Merchant Warehouse.

Payment gateway providers develop computer-based systems that facilitate the processing of transactions over the Internet. Payment gateways encrypt sensitive cardholder information to ensure that information passes securely between the parties involved.

There are many different payment gateway providers in the marketplace offering unique products and different levels of service. Payment gateway providers will typically use the same ISO sales channel that acquirers/processors use to get their product in front of the ultimate customer. Payment gateways are required for all ecommerce transactions as well as certain POS and custom hardware transactions.

Step-by-Step Electronic Payment Process

So now that you have a better idea of the terms used in the industry and who the key players are that participate in a transaction, it is time to go through a typical transaction from beginning to end.

Here is the scenario:

- James is a banking client of ABC Issuing Bank.

- ABC Issuing Bank has provided James with a premier rewards credit card because he is such a good customer and they would like him to have additional buying power in the marketplace.

- James goes shopping at a golf store called Super Golf in his hometown.

- Super Golf has established a merchant account with DEF Acquiring Bank and DEF Processor as part of their ordinary business process, and they are all set up to accept credit and debit cards from their customers.

James has been meaning to buy a few new golf shirts for the big golf trip he has finally gotten around to planning. He picks out his golf shirts and takes them up to the checkout counter. The salesperson behind the counter rings up his order and informs James that he owes $110.

The electronic payment process begins.

Step 1:

James takes out his ABC Issuing Bank premier rewards credit card because he really wants to earn those double bonus points.

James hands his credit card to the Super Golf employee who swipes the credit card through the credit card terminal sitting next to the register. The credit card terminal will do one of the following:

- dial out of the store using a standard phone line;

- transmit over an Internet-based (IP) line; or
- communicate wirelessly through a cellular connection.

Step 2:

James's transaction information, including the amount of the transaction and his credit card number, travels over the DEF Processor network to DEF Acquiring Bank.

Step 3:

DEF Acquiring Bank receives James's information about the purchase and sends out an authorization request to ABC Issuing Bank to find out if James has enough credit on his account to approve the transaction. (If James had used his debit card, the authorization request would have been made to see if he had enough money in his checking account to cover the purchase.)

Step 4:

ABC Issuing Bank

- provides an approval for the transaction;
- puts the $110 on hold at their bank; and
- sends an authorization response and authorization code back to DEF Acquiring Bank.

Step 5:

DEF Acquiring Bank sends the authorization code back to Super Golf, and James's customer receipt is printed out for him to sign. James signs his credit card receipt, and he is on his way.

That all sounds very time consuming and like a lot of work, but we all know from our own experiences that steps 1 through 5 can take as little as two seconds and typically no more than ten seconds, which really isn't long at all.

Over the course of the day, Super Golf performs hundreds of transactions with customers who use their credit or debit cards to pay for their purchases. Each of those credit and debit cards had been issued to these customers by different issuing banks. The process for each transaction is exactly the same for each customer, and at the end of the day Super Golf has $25,000 worth of sales that were all paid by credit or debit cards.

In order for Super Golf to get its money, the store must perform a batch settlement.

Step 6:

The manager of Super Golf performs a batch settlement on all credit card terminals in the store. A receipt is printed out for the company's financial records, and each of the authorization codes is sent back to DEF Acquiring Bank over the DEF Processor network.

Step 7:

DEF Acquiring Bank receives the authorization codes from Super Golf and now has to go out and collect the funds from each of the many issuing banks on behalf of its client (Super Golf).

Remember that, when the transactions were originally approved, each of the issuing banks put funds on hold. Now they are just waiting for DEF Acquiring Bank to come back and request a transfer of those funds.

Step 8:

Funds are transferred from each issuing bank to DEF Acquiring Bank, and DEF Acquiring Bank uses the ABA routing number provided by Super Golf during the application process to perform an ACH transfer of the $25,000 into Super Golf's business bank account.

When Super Golf's merchant account was set up, Super Golf was informed how long it would take from the time they performed their batch settlement to the time when their funds would be deposited into their bank account.

With certain acquiring banks/processors, next business day funding is provided as long as the batch settlement occurs by a specific time of day. With other acquiring banks, two- or three-day funding is provided.

Brick and Mortar vs. Internet

Super Golf's Internet-based sales happen a bit differently, utilizing a payment gateway that facilitates the transfer of information between Super Golf's website and the acquiring bank/processor. When a customer orders a product from the Super Golf website, the payment gateway performs a variety of tasks to process the transaction:

- A customer places an order on Super Golf's website by pressing the submit order or equivalent button.

- The customer's web browser encrypts the information to be sent between the browser and the merchant's web server. This is done via SSL encryption, which protects the customer's credit or debit card information.

- The web server then forwards the transaction details to its payment gateway (this is another SSL encrypted connection to the payment server hosted by the payment gateway).

- The payment gateway forwards the transaction information to the processor used by the merchant's acquiring bank (also encrypted).

- In a manner similar to a card-present transaction that was described earlier, the acquiring bank forwards the transaction information to the issuing bank for approval.

- The issuing bank receives the authorization request and sends a response back to the acquiring bank/processor (via the same process as the request for authorization) with an authorization response and authorization code.

- The processor forwards the response to the payment gateway.

- The payment gateway receives the response and forwards it on to Super Golf's website where it is interpreted as a relevant response and relayed back to the cardholder and the merchant.

- The entire process typically takes two to three seconds. The merchant submits all of its approved authorizations in a batch settlement to its acquiring bank for settlement.

- The acquiring bank obtains the funds from the various issuing banks and the acquiring bank deposits the total of the approved funds into the merchant's designated bank account.

In summary, the entire process of conducting electronic payments includes many parties and a significant amount of data being transferred. There is substantial money spent at the acquiring bank/processor on information technology, as well as at the issuing bank to ensure a secure and timely transaction response as well as a secure and efficient way to transfer the required funds. The customer only sees a small portion of the actual transaction process.

It is important for all merchants to fully understand how the process works and what goes on after they swipe a customer's card so they have a basis for how the pricing of their credit and debit card account is determined.

CHAPTER 2
What Is Interchange, and Why Do You Care about It?

This chapter will discuss

- the concept of interchange and why it is important;
- examples of interchange categories; and
- additional interchange fees.

If you have been in business for a while and accept credit and debit cards from your customers, you have in all likelihood heard the term *interchange*. If you have a merchant services provider that is transparent with how they conduct their business, you may have also received a very logical explanation of interchange.

In many instances, that is not the case. Merchants are often told not to worry about interchange and that the pricing they are being provided is "the best they can get given their business."

So what in the world is interchange, and why do you care about it?

As a merchant utilizing a merchant account, interchange and interchange fees play a critical role in how your monthly credit and debit card fees are calculated. That might not have been told to you by your merchant services salesperson, but *the concept of interchange is the most important factor in determining what you pay and what the merchant services provider makes on any transaction.*

Interchange fee is a term used in the payment card industry to describe a fee paid between banks for the acceptance of card-based transactions. Usually it is a fee that the acquiring bank pays to the issuing bank.

The interchange fee consists of both a discount rate component and a transaction fee component.

In a credit or debit card transaction, the issuing bank deducts the interchange fee from the amount it pays the acquiring bank that handles a credit or debit card transaction for their merchant. The acquiring bank then pays the merchant the amount of the transaction minus both the interchange fee and an additional smaller fee for the MSP.

Interchange fees are set by the card associations and are the *largest fee component* that merchants pay for the privilege of accepting credit and debit cards, representing up to 90 percent of the total merchant services fees by some estimates.

Interchange fees have a complex pricing structure, which is based on

- the card brand (Visa, MasterCard, Discover);
- regions or jurisdictions (within the United States or outside the United States);
- the type of credit or debit card (standard, reward, corporate card);
- the type and size of the accepting merchant; and
- the type of transaction (card-present or card-not-present).

There are over three hundred interchange categories for Visa, MasterCard, and Discover.

Each and every credit and debit card in the market falls into one of the hundreds of interchange categories designated by the card associations.

Examples of Visa interchange categories and interchange fees as of October 2011 include the following (rates and transaction fees obtained from Visa.com website http://usa.visa.com/merchants/operations/interchange_rates.html):

- **Visa CPS/Retail (credit)**
  - ○ 1.54 percent/$0.10 per transaction
  - ○ Traditional nonrewards card/card-present swiped transaction
- **Visa CPS/Card-Not-Present (credit)**
  - ○ 1.80 percent/$0.10 per transaction
  - ○ Traditional nonrewards card/card-not-present transaction
- **Visa CPS/Retail (regulated debit)**
  - ○ 0.05 percent/$0.21 per transaction
  - ○ Traditional nonrewards card/card-present or card-not-present transaction
- **Visa CPS/Rewards 1 (credit)**
  - ○ 1.65 percent/$0.10 per transaction
  - ○ Consumer traditional rewards card/card-present swiped transaction
- **Visa CPS/Rewards 2 (credit)**
  - ○ 1.95 percent/$0.10 per transaction
  - ○ Consumer traditional rewards card/card-not-present transaction
- **Visa CPS/Small Ticket (credit)**
  - ○ 1.65 percent/$0.04 per transaction
  - ○ Transaction balance less than $15
- **Visa Business Retail (credit)**
  - ○ 2.20 percent/$0.10 per transaction
  - ○ Business, signature business, corporate, or purchasing cards/card-present swiped transaction

For a complete listing of Visa and MasterCard interchange categories and interchange fees, please visit:

- http://usa.visa.com/merchants/operations/interchange _rates.html

- http://www.mastercard.com/us/merchant/support /interchange_rates.html

Interchange fees are established at differing levels for a variety of reasons. Some basic explanations of the types of interchange fees by card type are below:

- Debit cards represent a lower risk than credit cards and therefore have a lower interchange fee.

  - The simple reason for this is because with a debit card purchase, the customer's bank account is debited for the amount of the purchase, and if there isn't enough money in the bank account the transaction will not obtain an approval.

- A premium credit card that offers rewards generally will have a higher interchange fee than do standard credit cards with no rewards.

  - Yes, all of those great rewards programs are funded by the merchant.

  - If your customer uses a rewards credit card, you as the merchant are paying more in fees to accept that card.

- Sales that are not conducted in person (card-not-present) generally are subject to higher interchange fees than are card-present transactions.

  - This is based on the overall risk profile of taking a credit or debit card transaction without the ability to verify that the card actually belongs to the customer.

So what does all this mean?

In its simplest form, interchange fees are the *pure cost* to every acquiring bank providing their customers the ability to accept credit and debit cards. Interchange fees are completely unavoidable; regardless of how big or small the merchant and interchange fees play the most critical role in how your merchant account is priced.

Now you know what the cost of goods are for any merchant services provider.

This is very important and worth repeating:

The interchange fee is the pure cost to every acquiring bank and is completely unavoidable.

In addition to the discount rate and transaction fee for each specific type of card, there are various other interchange fees that are part of the pure cost to process a credit or debit card transaction. *Not all of these additional interchange fees will be incurred by every merchant.* These other fees include the following and are public information provided by Visa and MasterCard:

- **Visa Assessment:** fee assessed on the dollar amount of all Visa transactions
- **Visa International Service Assessments (ISA):** applies to all transactions where the merchant is located in the United States and the issuing bank is located outside the United States
- **Visa International Acquirer Fee (IAF) High Risk:** fee assessed on all transactions at a US merchant location with a non-US-issued card for high risk merchants in direct marketing
- **Visa Zero Dollar Verification Message:** fee assessed on all account verification messages, including both approved and declined as well as AVS account verification transactions. Account verification transactions must be submitted for $0 and are used to validate cardholder account numbers and other elements such as CVV2 and AVS prior to obtaining an actual authorization.
- **Visa Authorization Misuse Fee:** fee assessed on all authorized Visa transactions, which are not followed by a matching Visa clearing transaction (or not reversed in the case of a cancelled transaction)

- **Visa Zero Floor Limit Fee:** fee assessed on all Visa clearing transactions that are not authorized
- **Visa Network Acquirer Processing Fee:** fee assessed on all Visa authorization attempts. Does not apply to $0 account verification messages. *
- **Visa Partial Authorization Nonparticipation Fee:** fee assessed on automated fuel dispenser transactions that do not support partial authorizations
- **Visa Base II:** network transmission fee from Visa assessed to a bank on each transaction
- **Visa Risk:** third-party pass-through fee from Visa
- **MasterCard Assessment:** fee assessed on the dollar amount of all MasterCard signature debit transactions and MasterCard consumer and commercial credit transactions
- **MasterCard Cross Border:** fee assessed on the dollar amount of all MasterCard consumer credit, consumer debit, and commercial transaction records and credit records that are processed with the country code of the merchant being different from the country code of the cardholder
- **MasterCard Network Access and Brand Usage (NABU) Fee:** fee assessed on all MasterCard consumer credit, consumer debit, and commercial card sales and credit (return) transactions that are processed with a US-issued card at a US merchant
- **MasterCard Address Verification Service Fee, Card-Present:** fee assessed on all MasterCard card-present authorizations that use the address verification service and are submitted for more than $0
- **MasterCard Address Verification Service Fee, Card-Not-Present:** fee assessed on all MasterCard card-not-present authorizations that use the address verification service and are submitted for more than $0
- **MasterCard Account Status Inquiry Fee:** fee assessed on all account status inquiry services

- **MasterCard Processing Integrity Fee:** fee assessed on all MasterCard authorized transactions, which are not followed by a matching MasterCard clearing transaction (or not reversed in the case of a cancelled transaction)
- **MasterCard Settle:** a network transmission fee from MasterCard assessed to the bank

These additional fees are another basic cost to the MSP and are always accounted for when pricing a merchant account.

* Effective April 1, 2012, Visa implemented a new Fixed Acquirer Network Fee (FANF) which may vary each month and is based on the number of merchant locations. In addition, Visa reduced the current Network Acquirer Processing Fee (NAPF) from $0.0195 per authorization request to $0.0155 per authorization request for Visa debit card products. The current NAPF of $0.0195 remains unchanged for Visa credit card products.

All transaction related examples in this book do not take into account the changes made by Visa on April 1, 2012.

CHAPTER 3
Who Makes What on Each Transaction?

Now that you know what interchange is, it is time to understand which parties are making money (and how much) on each and every credit and debit card transaction.

This chapter will discuss

- the entities that make money on credit and debit card transactions;
- what they make; and
- how the amount they make is calculated.

Issuing Bank

We all know that issuing banks make money by charging their customers interest when the credit card balance is not paid in full at the end of the month.

Now you also know that issuing banks make money from the interchange fee each and every time their client uses that credit or debit card to make a purchase.

Interchange fees provide issuing banks billions of dollars in revenue every year.

Here is an example of a single transaction:

Transaction Amount	$100
Interchange Category	VISA CPS/Rewards 2
Interchange Discount Rate	1.95 percent
Interchange Transaction Fee	$0.10
Total Interchange Fee Paid to Issuing Bank	$2.05 [($100 x 1.95 percent) + $0.10]
Actual Percentage of Transaction Amount	2.05 percent ($2.05/$100)

Now that might not seem like a lot of money, but don't forget this is just one single transaction. Think about how often consumers use their credit and debit cards to make everyday purchases; these numbers add up very quickly.

Card Associations

Visa, MasterCard, and Discover are major players in today's financial markets and have significant revenue to show for it. Without the vast networks created by these important companies, today's electronic payment process would not exist.

The card associations make money from two different sources:

1. **Assessments**

   Part of the other fees that were discussed at the end of chapter 2, assessment fees are set by Visa, MasterCard, and Discover, respectively. These fees are uniform across the industry and are another pure cost to any MSP.

a. **Visa:** currently 0.11 percent (11 basis points) on the dollar amount of all Visa transactions

b. **MasterCard:** currently 0.11 percent (11 basis points) on the dollar amount of all MasterCard transactions less than $1,000 and 0.12 percent (12 basis points) on the dollar amount of all MasterCard transactions greater than or equal to $1,000

c. **Discover:** currently 0.10 percent (10 basis points) on the dollar amount of all Discover transactions

2. **Network Fees (as of October 1, 2011)**

These are additional fees for all authorization attempts made on the respective card association network.

a. **Visa (NAPF):** currently $0.0195 per authorization attempt

b. **MasterCard (NABU):** currently $0.0185 per authorization attempt

c. **Discover (Discover Usage Fee):** currently $0.0185 per authorization attempt

Every transaction made with a Visa, MasterCard, or Discover credit or debit card will incur an assessment fee and a network fee.

Acquirers, Processors, ISOs, and Banks (MSPs)

Here is where things get interesting and why merchant services fees have become very difficult for the average person to understand.

There are clear financial reasons why an issuing bank and the card associations want you to use your credit or debit card to make purchases. They are all detailed above.

The issuing bank and the card associations are *not* the ones that market and sell merchant accounts. That job belongs to the MSPs, or some combination thereof. And of course, they make money too.

The fee paid to the MSP is the only piece of merchant account pricing that is negotiable and somewhat in the merchant's control.

In order to be able to negotiate a good deal, you have to know how it all works.

Prior to discussing the various pricing methods in the next chapter, you need to understand some background about MSPs and an explanation as to how they often work together.

Acquiring Bank/Processors

As stated in the Nilsson Report in March 2010, the ten largest merchant processing acquiring banks are the following:

1. First Data
2. Bank of America
3. Fifth Third Bank
4. Chase Paymentech
5. Heartland Payments
6. RBS WorldPay
7. Elavon
8. Global Payments
9. Wells Fargo
10. FNMS

As you look at this list you might be wondering which of these entities are acquiring banks and which are processors. Acquiring banks need a processor, and processors need an acquiring bank.

Think back to chapter 1 and how the electronic payment process works.

- The data moves over the processor's network to the acquiring bank and then to the issuing bank for authorization.

- It is critical that acquiring banks and processors team together.

Answering the question raised above, the names of the companies with which you would traditionally open a bank account are the acquiring banks; the ones you may not have ever heard of are the processors.

Each of these entities has a direct sales channel that sells merchant services into the marketplace. They also build strategic alliances with each other to achieve the best financial results for their organizations.

Since interchange fees are actually being allocated at this level, the pure cost to these entities to process a credit or debit card transaction is only the base interchange fee (discount rate and transaction fee), including assessments from the card associations, the card associations network fees, and any other interchange fees applicable to a transaction.

In other words, these entities have the absolute lowest buy rate or cost of goods when it comes to selling merchant services to their customers.

ISO

As a quick refresher, an ISO is a company that independently solicits potential merchants on behalf of an acquirer/processor. Think of an ISO as an independent frontend sales organization or reseller for an acquirer/processor.

ISOs have an agreed-upon buy rate with one or more acquiring banks/processors that will be equal to interchange fees *plus something*. That "something" can be in the form of basis points (a small percentage of the transaction amount) and/or a transaction fee (swipe fee).

For example, ISO XYZ could have a buy rate from their acquiring bank/processor of 2 basis points (0.02 percent) and $0.05 over interchange (the interchange fees). ISO XYZ can then sell processing to merchants at any price they want over that set buy rate. The ISO agreement between the acquirer/processor and the ISO will also state what the revenue split will be on the ultimate price to the merchant over the buy rate, which can range from 50 to 100 percent depending on the deal.

For ISO XYZ, the first 2 basis points and $0.05 of every transaction that their clients conduct would go to the acquirer/processor and anything over and above that amount would go to ISO XYZ (assuming a 100 percent/0 percent split).

Having an ISO or a middleman on a deal is often a good thing for the merchant:

- There are many ISOs in the market that will actually provide better pricing than the acquiring bank/processors would charge directly, simply because they are willing to make less on a deal and they have a lower base overhead cost.

- ISOs will typically handle their own customer service, providing a convenience to their clients of making one phone call when issues arise. The ISO will field the initial customer service call and handle all aspects of the resolution process on behalf of its client.

- You just have to find the right ISO to work with.

In order to be able to market merchant accounts, an ISO must be sponsored by an acquiring bank. This sponsorship requires that the acquiring bank verify the financial stability and suitability of the ISO that will be marketing on its behalf. The ISO must also pay a fee to be registered with Visa and MasterCard and must comply with regulations as to how it may market merchant accounts and the use of copyrights of Visa and MasterCard.

One way for a merchant to verify if an ISO is in compliance is to check the ISO's website or any other marketing material for a disclosure reading something like "XYZ company is a registered ISO/MSP of [bank, town, state]." This disclosure is required by both Visa and MasterCard, and an ISO will incur a fine of up to $25,000 if the disclosure is not clearly visible. In almost all cases, if there is no disclosure the company is likely to be an uninformed fourth party or worse. In many cases unregistered operators putting themselves out as registered ISOs have been responsible for some of the worst horror stories in merchant services.

Banks

We are all familiar with the many big-name banking institutions in the United States as well as many smaller local and regional banks. This is a logical place for you, as a merchant, to look for help with your merchant account. Why not? You already have a relationship with the bank via a checking account, a certificate of deposit, a line of credit, or some other financial product. With larger businesses, these banking relationships can be significant.

Banks large and small use these key customer relationships to best position themselves to obtain their customers merchant account business. Given the relationship between the bank and the merchant, you would expect to get the best possible merchant account pricing deal from your bank and not ever have to look elsewhere.

Unfortunately, that is not always the case, and banks will often use their existing relationship to their advantage when it comes to pricing a merchant account.

The majority of banks have a strategic partnership with one of the many large processors in the country. The terms of those relationships are not public record, but one would assume that if the bank is big enough and has a large enough client base (i.e., business clients), the acquiring bank/processor will provide a very attractive buy rate to the bank as the basis for their merchant services pricing.

In many instances, that buy rate will be straight interchange fees exactly like the acquiring bank/processor has when it solicits business through its own in-house sales channel.

Once again, these banks will likely have the absolute lowest buy rate or cost of goods when it comes to selling merchant services to their customers.

CHAPTER 4
Pricing Strategies and Additional Fees: The Real Truth

It is now time for the chapter you have all been waiting for. I'm sure you've been wondering, "How exactly is my merchant account priced, and how can I get a better deal?"

This chapter will discuss

- the many pricing components of your merchant account;
- popular pricing strategies; and
- additional fees to be aware of.

Remember:

- Interchange fees are set by the card associations and are the largest component of the various fees that a merchant pays for the privilege of accepting credit and debit cards.
- Interchange fees have complex pricing structures.

There are hundreds of interchange categories that have been created by the card associations, each having a different *discount rate* and *transaction fee* (described in chapter 2).

A common Visa interchange category is **Visa CPS/Rewards 2,** which includes traditional rewards, signature, and infinite cards in a card-not-present transaction. This interchange category would be obtained if the credit card used by the customer was a rewards card and the transaction was hand-keyed into a credit card terminal (card-not-present).

Going back to our example from chapter 3, the **Visa CPS/Rewards 2** interchange category has a discount rate of 1.95 percent and a $0.10 transaction fee.

The transaction amount is $100.

Table 4.1: Basic Interchange Fee Example

Interchange Category	Interchange Discount Rate	Interchange Transaction Fee	Assessment	Network Fee	Total Interchange Fee
	(A)	(B)	(C)	(D)	(E)
Visa CPS/ Rewards 2	1.95 percent	$0.10	0.11 percent	$0.0195	$2.18
How $ amount is calculated	$1.95 ($100 transaction amount x 1.95 percent)		$0.11 ($100 transaction amount x 0.11 percent)		$1.95 + $0.10 + $0.11 + $0.0195

How to read Table 4.1

(A) **Interchange discount rate:** public information published by the card associations

(B) **Interchange transaction fee:** public information published by the card associations

(C) **Assessment:** fee paid to Visa

(D) **Network fee:** fee paid to Visa

(E) **Total interchange fee:** $1.95 (A) + $0.10 (B) + $0.11 (C) + $0.0195 (D) = $2.18 or 2.18 percent on the $100 transaction

The most important thing to understand about the total interchange fee is that in order to process a payment, all MSP's have this base overhead cost.

This is the *pure cost of processing* for any MSP.

What every merchant needs to know is:

- how much they are paying over and above the pure cost of processing, or
- how much over the interchange fees is their merchant account being priced.

With this in mind you are now ready to understand merchant services pricing.

Pricing strategies employed by MSPs can vary significantly.

- The merchant processing industry has taken the base interchange fee or pure cost of processing and wrapped it up into a pretty package to market to potential customers.
- There are three standard pricing methods in the market today.
- The simpler a pricing proposal sounds, the less likely it is that you are getting the most advantageous pricing method for you and your business.
- Remember, your main objective as a merchant is to know exactly what you are paying over and above the pure cost of processing.

You will see that only one of the pricing methods called interchange or cost-plus pricing makes the most sense for all merchants regardless of their size.

The three types of standard pricing in the market are these:

1. Fixed-rate pricing
2. Multi-tier or three-tier pricing
3. Interchange or cost-plus pricing

Fixed-Rate Pricing

On its face, fixed-rate pricing appears to be a very straightforward way to price a merchant account.

- The salesperson tells you that your rate is going to be 1.60 percent, and when you compare that rate to what you are currently paying, it sounds great.

- Each and every Visa, MasterCard, and Discover transaction will be charged the 1.60 percent rate, but there will also be additional *downgrade* fees applied to a large percentage of your monthly transactions.

- Downgrade fees are typically not part of your sales conversation, nor is how much your all-in rate will differ from that promised fixed rate of 1.60 percent.

So, what is a downgrade fee, and what can you do about it?

- A downgrade occurs when the credit or debit card used by your customer has an interchange discount rate higher than the low fixed rate that was offered on your account.

- In certain instances, downgrades will apply even when the interchange discount rate is lower than the fixed rate that was offered.

- Downgrades are common with fixed-rate pricing when a rewards card or corporate card is used by the customer.

- The downgrade fee will also include a profit margin for the MSP, which is not told to the merchant or disclosed on your monthly statement.

Going back to our example with the **Visa CPS/Rewards 2** credit card:

The transaction amount is $100.

Table 4.2: Fixed-Rate Pricing Example

Interchange Category	Interchange Discount Rate	Fixed Rate Sold to Merchant	Loss to MSP	Profit Margin to MSP	Total Downgrade
	(A)	(B)	(C)	(D)	
Visa CPS/ Rewards 2	1.95 percent	1.60 percent	0.35 percent	1.00 percent	1.35 percent
			(1.95 percent −1.60 percent)	Ranges b/w 0.50 percent −2.00 percent	(C) + (D)

How to read Table 4.2

(A) **Interchange discount rate:** public information published by the card associations

(B) **Fixed rate sold to merchant:** that low rate promised to the merchant by the merchant services salesperson

(C) **Loss to MSP:** Think of this as buying goods at 1.95 percent and selling them at 1.60 percent. That is a loss no matter how you calculate it.

(D) **Profit margin to MSP:** profit to merchant services provider. This can range from 0.50 to 2.00 percent. For this example, we will assume a profit margin of 1.00 percent.

The *all-in rate* for this card type and this specific transaction is 2.95 percent. The merchant services provider margin is 1.00 percent.

- The fixed rate (1.60 percent) is added to the total downgrade from Table 4.2 above (1.35 percent). The transaction that was supposed to occur at a rate of 1.60 percent now has an all-in rate of 2.95 percent.

- *So much for 1.60 percent.*

You will typically see the following items on your monthly statement:

- a summary section of all Visa, MasterCard, and Discover transactions with a column entitled discount rate;
- a discount rate column, which will have the 1.60 percent clearly listed along with the associated dollar fee for each type of card; and
- a listing of additional fees. (Typically toward the end, you will see other fees listed with names on the left side that do not make much sense. These are the specific interchange categories your customer's transactions qualified for.)

In our example, using a $100 transaction, you would see this at the end of the monthly statement:

Other Fees:

Interchange Category	Transaction Amt	Fee
Visa CPS/Rewards 2	$100	$1.35

Using this information you can calculate your all-in rate for each of the card types:

- Divide the $1.35 by $100 to get 1.35 percent. This is the downgrade percentage.
- Add the 1.35 percent to your fixed rate of 1.60 percent for a total of 2.95 percent.

Your all-in rate for that specific card type is 2.95 percent.

It is not impossible to figure out what the all-in rate is for each card type, however:

- Your merchant account statement will not make it easy.
- On certain statements, you will only see the interchange category, the number of transactions, and the total

downgrade fee, making it even more difficult to back into the all-in rate.

○ If you don't have the transaction amount ($) on your statement, then you will need to calculate an average ticket (look back to the industry terms in chapter 1) for the specific card brand (Visa, MasterCard, and Discover) and multiply that average ticket amount by the number of transactions to find the dollar amount used to calculate the additional downgrade fee.

The information is usually all there on your monthly statement, but unless you know what everything means and how to put the puzzle together, it can be an extremely scary and near-impossible task.

Multi-Tier or Three-Tier Pricing

This is probably the most common pricing method in the industry today. The MSP takes the hundreds of interchange categories and puts them into multiple buckets or groups.

Typically there are three buckets: *qualified, mid-qualified, nonqualified.* Each bucket will have a different fixed rate associated with it. For example:

- **Qualified rate:** 1.50 percent
- **Mid-qualified rate:** 2.50 percent
- **Nonqualified rate:** 3.50 percent

A few things to understand:

1. The specific interchange categories in each bucket are not disclosed to the merchant, nor does the merchant have any say in how those buckets are created.

2. The fixed rate for each bucket is set by the MSP.

   If a client calls and asks for a price reduction, the merchant services provider will simply reduce the rate of one or more of the buckets by a small amount. It might sound like a nice gesture, but it usually doesn't provide any significant cost savings for the merchant.

3. Most important, there will never be a card type placed in a bucket with an interchange discount rate higher than the fixed rate assigned to that bucket.

The simple reason for all this is that merchant services providers never lose money.

Qualified Rate (Qual.)

The qualified rate is the percentage rate a merchant will be charged whenever it accepts a regular consumer credit or debit card or processes a card in a manner defined as "standard" by the merchant services provider using an approved credit card processing solution. In addition, keep in mind the following:

- The qualified rate is usually the lowest rate a merchant will incur when accepting a credit or debit card from a customer.

- The qualified rate is the rate commonly quoted to a merchant when it inquires about pricing.

- The qualified rate is created based on the way a merchant will be accepting a majority of its credit and debit card transactions.

- For an Internet merchant account, the Internet interchange categories will be defined as qualified.

- For a physical retailer only transactions swiped through the credit card terminal in an ordinary manner will be defined as qualified.

While a 1.50 percent qualified rate sounds like a good deal, a merchant needs to ask this simple question:

- Are we accepting a large number of debit cards from our clients?

Starting in October 2011 following the implementation of the Durbin Amendment, the majority of debit cards have an interchange fee of 0.05 percent (5 basis points) plus $0.21 per transaction. In some instances the transaction fee will be $0.22, but the fee of 5 basis points remains in place.

There is a big difference between a qualified rate of 1.50 percent that the merchant will always pay and an interchange fee discount rate of 0.05 percent (remember, this is the pure cost of processing): 1.45 percent to be exact.

What does this all mean?

It means the merchant services provider is making a little less than 1.50 percent on all regulated debit card transactions that occur with a merchant having a 1.50 percent qualified rate. That is a very large margin in the world of merchant processing.

Mid-Qualified Rate (Mid-qual.)

The mid-qualified rate is the percentage rate a merchant will be charged whenever it accepts a credit or debit card that does not qualify for the lowest rate (qualified rate). This may happen for several reasons, including the following:

- A consumer credit or debit card is keyed into a credit card terminal instead of being swiped.

- A special kind of credit card (such as a rewards card or business card) is used by the customer.

Merchants priced on three-tier pricing will typically see a larger percentage of mid-qualified rate credit and debit cards than qualified rate credit and debit cards on their merchant account statement.

It will be easy to know based upon how you conduct your business whether reason one above is why the transaction is "not qualifying." Identifying when reason two is the culprit is not always as obvious.

Everyone loves rewards cards.

Think about all of the different rewards cards out there in the marketplace. Remember all of the commercials on TV about reward card programs. Now look in your wallet. The majority of credit and even debit cards all have a rewards program attached to them. Once a reward program is affiliated with a card, say good-bye to the qualified rate.

A mid-qualified rate in three-tier pricing is higher than a qualified rate simply because card types/transactions that are grouped into the mid-qualified bucket will cost the MSP more in base interchange fees (their cost), so the rates to the merchant are increased.

Nonqualified Rate (Nonqual.)

The nonqualified rate is usually the highest percentage rate a merchant will be charged whenever it accepts a credit or debit card. All transactions that are not qualified or mid-qualified will fall to this nonqualified rate category. This may happen for several reasons, including the following:

- A consumer credit or debit card is keyed into a credit card terminal instead of being swiped, and address verification is not performed.

- A special kind of credit or debit card is used like a business card and all required fields are not entered.

- A merchant does not settle its daily batch within the allotted time frame, usually forty-eight hours from the time of authorization.

Back to our $100 example with a **Visa CPS/Rewards 2**.

Table 4.3: Multi-Tier Pricing Example

Interchange Category	Interchange Discount Rate	Bucket Chosen by MSP	Rate on Mid-qual. and Nonqual. Buckets	Cost to MSP (interchange fee)	Profit to MSP
	(A)		(B)	(C)	
Visa CPS/ Rewards 2	1.95 percent	Mid-qual.	2.50 percent	2.18 percent	**0.32 percent**
		Nonqual.	3.50 percent	2.18 percent	**1.32 percent**
				Table 4.1	(B) – (C)

How to read Table 4.3

(A) **Interchange discount rate:** public information published by the card associations

(B) **Rate on mid-qualified and nonqualified buckets:** the discount rate the merchant will pay for this card type (calculated on the dollar amount of the transaction)

(C) **Cost to MSP (interchange fee):** Refer to Table 4.1.

(D) **Profit to MSP:** the rate charged to the merchant (B) minus the cost to MSP (C)

Which bucket do you think this card type would be put into? My guess would be nonqualified.

As you can see:

- The amount the MSP makes over and above the pure interchange fee is different depending on how the buckets are set up and the discount rate for each bucket.
- The margin is also dependent on the type of card used by the customer. Some cards are more profitable to the MSP, and some are not.

Wouldn't it be nice to know that your merchant services provider is making the same amount on each transaction regardless of the type of credit or debit card your customer uses to make their purchase?

It is absolutely possible but you need to know what to ask for.

Interchange or Cost-Plus Pricing

Interchange or cost-plus pricing has historically been offered to only large merchants that do a lot of transactions with high monthly dollar volumes. Larger merchants will typically have more leverage to negotiate with the MSP and are able to get better pricing.

With smaller merchants, there are many MSPs that try to convince the merchant that interchange or cost-plus pricing is not the best way for them to be priced, and they are steered toward fixed-rate or three-tier pricing; but ...

... nothing could be further from the truth!

With interchange or cost-plus pricing

- the interchange fees (pure cost of processing) are passed directly through to the merchant; and
- the MSP adds a small percentage and transaction fee above and beyond that pure cost.

An example of interchange or cost-plus pricing would be for a merchant to be priced as follows:

Interchange + 0.20 percent (20 basis points) and $0.10 per transaction

This means that regardless of the type of credit or debit card a customer uses to make a purchase, the merchant knows with 100 percent certainty that the fee it will pay over and above the pure interchange fees is always the same: 20 basis points (0.20 percent) and $0.10 per transaction.

Don't forget that pure cost will be different depending on the type of credit or debit card used. This part is beyond anyone's control.

Back to our $100 example with a **Visa CPS/Rewards 2**.

Table 4.4: Interchange or Cost-Plus Pricing Example

Interchange Category	Interchange Discount Rate	Assessment/ Network Fee	Interchange Fee, Passed Through to Merchant	Fee to MSP	Total Cost to Merchant
	(A)	(B)	(C)	(D)	(E)
Visa CPS/ Rewards 2	1.95 percent	0.11 percent/ $0.0195	$2.18	0.20 percent ($0.20) + $0.10	**$2.48**
			Table 4.1	**Total of $0.30**	$2.18 + $0.30

How to read Table 4.4

(A) **Interchange discount rate:** public information published by the card associations

(B) **Assessment/network fee:** fees paid to Visa

(C) **Interchange fee, passed through to merchant:** the pass-through interchange fee (Table 4.1)

(D) **Fee to MSP:** (0.20 percent × $100) + $0.10 = $0.30

(E) **Total cost to merchant:** $2.18 (C) + $0.30 (D) = $2.48 (2.48 percent all-in rate)

Interchange or cost plus pricing is the *only* way a merchant can know exactly what it is paying above and beyond interchange fees or the pure cost of processing.

Interchange or cost-plus pricing is the only transparent pricing method in the industry.

Which pricing method would you rather be on?

The Table below explains a $100 transaction using a **Visa CPS/ Rewards 2** credit card:

Table 4.5: Pricing Example Cost Comparison

Interchange Category	Cost to Merchant with Fixed-Rate Pricing (1.60 percent fixed rate)	Cost to Merchant with Three-Tier Pricing (assuming nonqualified bucket)	Cost to Merchant with Interchange PLUS Pricing (20 bps/$0.10)
	(A)	(B)	(C)
Visa CPS/ Rewards 2	$2.95 or a 2.95 percent all-in rate	$3.50 or a 3.50 percent all-in rate	$2.48 or a 2.48 percent all-in rate

Additional Fees

There are additional fees that are often charged on a merchant account that the merchant needs to be aware of. Not all merchant services providers charge these additional fees. When comparing providers, it is important to ask about these additional fees and know exactly if and when they will be applied to your account.

Nuisance Fees

- Nuisance fees are charged when a credit or debit card is declined and then swiped again; the result is this so-called nuisance fee for each additional swipe.
- This fee can be very costly to the merchant.
- Nuisance fees can be upward of twenty dollars per occurrence.

Authorization Fee

- Authorization fees (actually an authorization request fee) are charged each time a transaction is sent to the issuing bank for approval.
- This fee applies whether or not the transaction is actually approved.
- This is not the same as the transaction fee that is part of the base-cost interchange fee and disclosed on the card association public schedules.
- This is an amount that the MSP makes on each swipe or authorization request.
- Authorization fees can occur with all three types of pricing strategies that were previously discussed.
- It is typical to see an authorization fee on interchange or cost-plus pricing.

Statement Fee
- Statement fees are monthly fees associated with the monthly statement that is sent to the merchant at the end of each monthly processing cycle.
- The monthly statement shows how much processing was done by the merchant and the fees that were incurred.
- Often, the statement fee is not directly linked to paper statements but rather to general overhead of the MSP.

Monthly Minimum Fee
- A monthly minimum fee is a way to ensure that merchants pay a minimum amount in fees each month to cover the merchant services provider's costs of maintaining the account and to create minimal profits.
- If a merchant's overall fees to the MSP do not equal or exceed the monthly minimum fee, the merchant will be charged up to the monthly minimum fee to satisfy the monthly minimum fee requirement.

Here is an example: A merchant has signed a merchant agreement with a twenty-five-dollar monthly minimum fee. If all of the processing fees in a month only totals fifteen dollars, this merchant will be charged an additional ten dollars to meet their monthly minimum fee requirement. Sometimes there are fees that are charged that are not a part of the monthly minimum fee requirement, such as statement fees. It is industry standard to charge a monthly minimum fee; however, not all MSPs charge them to merchants.

Batch Fee
- A batch fee (also known as a batch header fee) is charged to a merchant whenever the merchant performs a batch settlement of its credit card terminal or POS system sending its completed transactions for the day to its acquiring bank for settlement and payment.
- Typically batch fees equal $0.25 per occurrence.

- Not all merchant services providers charge merchants a batch fee.

Customer Service Fee

- A customer service fee is charged by some merchant services providers to pay for the cost of customer service.

- This fee is also referred to as a merchant support fee, maintenance fee, or service fee by some merchant services providers.

Annual Fee

- The annual fee is charged by some merchant services providers to cover the costs of maintaining the merchant account.

- These fees can be assessed monthly, quarterly, or annually.

- Annual fees can range from $79 to $399 or more.

Non-PCI (Payment Card Industry) Compliance Fee

- This is a fee assessed on a monthly basis if a merchant is not PCI compliant (see chapter 6).

- It is easy to avoid this non-PCI compliance fee, but there are many merchants paying it on a monthly basis.

- Your merchant services provider should provide consultation about how to avoid these non-PCI compliance fees.

Early Termination Fee

- An early termination fee is charged by merchant services providers if the merchant terminates the merchant agreement before the end of the contract term.

- Contract terms typically range from three to five years; generally, advance notice of six months to one year is required to cancel, or the early termination fee will be assessed.

Early termination fees can be stated in many different ways:

- a flat fee regardless of when the contract is terminated;
- a tiered fee schedule with a higher fee assessed when the remaining contract term is longer; or
- a "lost profit" fee where the merchant services provider calculates the average profit it made during the prior months of the contract and multiplies that amount by the remaining months of the contract when the merchant decides to cancel.

Early termination fees are typically presented as the first two bullet points above. If your merchant agreement includes any form of the lost profit fee described above, it can become very costly to break the contract. In certain instances, depending on the volume of business a company does in a month, a lost profit early termination fee can be hundreds of thousands of dollars or more.

Chargeback Fee

- The chargeback is the largest risk that is presented to acquirers/processors. This is not to be confused with a refund, which is simply a merchant refunding a transaction to its customer.
- In the Visa, MasterCard, and Discover rules, the merchant's acquiring bank is 100 percent responsible for all the transactions that the merchant performs.
  - This can leave the acquiring bank open to millions of dollars in potential losses if the merchant operates in an illegal or risky manner and generates many chargebacks.
  - Merchant services providers pass this cost on to the merchant, but if the merchant is fraudulent or simply does not have the money, the merchant acquirer must pay all the costs to make the cardholder whole.
- Chargeback risk is the most important factor taken into consideration during the contract application and underwriting process.

- ○ Some acquiring banks are much more stringent than others when assessing a merchant's chargeback risk.
- If a merchant encounters a chargeback, the acquiring bank assesses a chargeback fee.
  - ○ Chargeback fees can range from five dollars to twenty-five dollars per chargeback regardless of the ultimate resolution.
- A potential chargeback is presented to the acquiring bank on behalf of the issuing bank.
  - ○ A reason code is established by the issuing bank to properly identify the type of chargeback based on the cardholder's complaint. The most common complaint is that the cardholder cannot remember the transaction that appeared on his or her monthly statement. Usually, these potential chargebacks are corrected when the issuing bank sends over more details about the transaction.
- In addition to a chargeback fee, some merchant services providers charge an additional fee for gathering information from the acquiring bank and merchant. This is known as a retrieval request.
- Currently both Visa and MasterCard require all merchants to maintain no more than 1 percent of dollar volume processed to be chargebacks. If the percentage goes above 1 percent, there are fines ranging from $5,000 to $25,000 to the merchant's acquiring bank and ultimately passed on to the merchant.

CHAPTER 5
My Month-End Statement Makes No Sense—Please Help!

The last chapter helped you better understand how the many pricing methods actually work. You are now ready to understand your merchant account statement.

This chapter will discuss

- how to read your monthly statement;
- statement examples for each of the three popular pricing strategies; and
- the right pricing strategy for your business.

Credit card processing fees can be a significant monthly cost for your organization, but if you can't make sense of the month-end statement, what good is it?

Imagine if you couldn't understand your bank-account statement and how your money was being accounted for?

This chapter will show you how to read a monthly statement under all three pricing methods. For each statement example, we will use the same transaction data, and you will be able to see exactly how different pricing methods 1) disclose different types of information and 2) cost the merchant different amounts.

Table 5.1 shows the number of transactions and the total dollar amount for each card type.

We will use these transaction amounts for all three of our statement examples.

Table 5.1: Statement Example Transaction Assumptions

Card Type	# Sales	$ Sales	# Credit	$ Credit	Net Sales
Visa	101	$19,353	0	$0	$19,353
MasterCard	69	$18,856	0	$0	$18,856
Discover	0	$0	0	$0	$0
Debit	32	$5,491	0	$0	$5,491
Total	**202**	**$43,700**	**0**	**$0**	**$43,700**

Table 5.2 shows the different interchange categories that each of the 202 transactions actually qualified for once the batch settlement occurred. The actual interchange fee (interchange discount rate and interchange transaction fee) is disclosed along with the assumed bucket the card category would fall into for three-tier pricing.

Table 5.2: Statement Example Transaction Detail

Interchange Category	# Sales	$ Sales	Interchange Discount Rate	Interchange Transaction Fee	Tier Applicable to Three-Tier Pricing
Visa Rewards 1	26	$6,053.70	1.65%	$0.10	Mid-qual.
Visa VSP Retail	1	$85.00	1.54%	$0.10	Mid qual.
MC Foreign Standard	1	$112.50	2.15%	$0.10	Nonqual.
Visa EIRF	3	$798.00	2.30%	$0.10	Nonqual.
MC Commercial Face to Face	1	$113.00	2.15%	$0.10	Nonqual.
MC Enhanced Merit I	1	$150.00	2.04%	$0.10	Nonqual.
MC Enhanced Merit III	22	$7,877.85	1.73%	$0.10	Mid-qual.
MC World Elite Merit 3	1	$104.00	2.20%	$0.10	Nonqual.
Visa CNP	1	$100.00	1.80%	$0.10	Mid-qual.
MC World Merit I	1	$350.00	2.08%	$0.10	Nonqual.
MC World Merit III	8	$2,979.00	1.73%	$0.10	Mid-qual.
Visa Business Elect	1	$300.00	2.40%	$0.10	Nonqual.
Visa Retail Credit	69	$12,016.30	1.54%	$0.10	Qual.
MC Retail Credit	34	$7,169.65	1.58%	$0.10	Qual.
Regulated Debit	32	$5,491	0.05%	$0.21	Qual.
Totals	**202**	**$43,700**			

Additional assumptions for all statement examples:

Visa and MasterCard Assessment: 0.11 percent of the dollar value of sales in the reporting month

Visa Network Fee (NAPF): $0.0195 per transaction

MasterCard Network (NABU): $0.0185 per transaction

MasterCard Cross Border Fee: 0.40 percent of the total dollar value of sales for the applicable transaction in the reporting month

Visa and MasterCard interchange discount rates and transaction fees in Table 5.2 are taken from the interchange schedules published October 1, 2011. These interchange fees take into account adjustments made pursuant to the Durbin Amendment that went into effect in October 2011.

We will need to make certain general assumptions for the purposes of explaining each of the three types of statements.

Fixed-Rate Pricing Assumptions:
- 1.83 percent qualified rate
- Downgrades will apply
- $0.10 transaction fee
- $10 statement fee
- $0.25 batch settlement fee per occurrence
- $19.95 PCI noncompliance fee

Three-Tier Pricing Assumptions:
- 1.50 percent qualified rate
- 2.50 percent mid-qualified rate
- 3.50 percent nonqualified rate
- $0.10 transaction fee
- $10 statement fee

- $0.25 batch settlement fee per occurrence
- $19.95 PCI noncompliance fee

Interchange or Cost-Plus Pricing Assumptions:

- Pricing at interchange PLUS 0.20 percent (20 basis points) and $0.10 per transaction
- $10 statement fee
- No batch settlement fee (merchant services providers that price with interchange or cost-plus pricing will typically not charge a batch-settlement fee)
- $19.95 PCI noncompliance fee

Fixed-Rate Pricing Statement (page 1)

Name of MSP

Address

Processing month: xx/xx

Merchant number: xxxxxxxxxxx

Merchant name

Address

Transaction Summary:

Congratulations, your Qualified Rate is 1.83%.

Table 5.3: Fixed-Rate Pricing Statement Transaction Summary

Card Type	# Sales	$ Sales	# Credit	$ Credit	Net Sales	Disc %	Trans Fee	Discount Due
Visa	101	$19,353	0	$0	$19,353	1.83%	**$0.00**	$354.16
Master Card	69	$18,856	0	$0	$18,856	1.83%	**$0.00**	$345.06
Discover	0	$0	0	$0	$0	1.83%	**$0.00**	$0
Debit	32	$5,491	0	$0	$5,491	0.80%	$0.10	$47.13
Total	**202**	**$43,700**	**0**	**$0**	**$43,700**			**$746.35**

Fixed-Rate Pricing Statement (page 2)

How to read Table 5.3

Card Type: type of credit or debit cards the customers used to make payments in the reporting month

 # Sales: number of sales for each card type in the reporting month

$ Sales: dollar value of sales for each card type in the reporting month

 # Credit: number of credits for each card type in the reporting month

$ Credit: dollar value of credits for each card type in the reporting month

Net Sales: dollar value of sales minus dollar value of credits for each card type in the reporting month

Disc %: the fixed rate that was quoted to the merchant (Each credit card transaction for each card type is assessed this fixed discount rate of 1.83 percent. Debit card transactions are assessed a fixed discount rate of 0.80 percent plus $0.10 per transaction.)

Trans Fee: the amount assessed on each transaction for each card type in the reporting month

Discount Due: calculated as (Net Sales × Disc %) + (# Sales × Trans Fee) for each card type

Take notice that for the Visa, MasterCard, and Discover credit card categories, there is no trans fee disclosed in Table 5.3. This could lead merchants to believe that they are just being charged the fixed rate of 1.83 percent.

That is not the case. Look at the downgrade information later on in the statement. *Watts authorization* and *debit authorization* are just different names for transaction fee.

Fixed-Rate Pricing Statement (page 3)

Batch Information:

Table 5.4: Fixed-Rate Pricing Statement Batch Summary

Day	Ref#	# Sales	$ Sales	# Credit	$ Credit	Net Deposit
01	111xxx	4	$430	0	$0	$430
03	111xxx	8	$977	0	$0	$977
03	111xxx	12	$2,141	0	$0	$2,141
05	111xxx	16	$3,523	0	$0	$3,523
06	111xxx	10	$2,604	0	$0	$2,604
06	111xxx	8	$1,031	0	$0	$1,031
08	111xxx	14	$2,784	0	$0	$2,784
10	111xxx	8	$2,883	0	$0	$2,883
12	111xxx	6	$1,773	0	$0	$1,773
13	111xxx	12	$3,049	0	$0	$3,049
15	111xxx	7	$1,369	0	$0	$1,369
17	111xxx	9	$1,357	0	$0	$1,357
17	111xxx	5	$703	0	$0	$703
19	111xxx	10	$2,801	0	$0	$2,801
20	111xxx	11	$3,193	0	$0	$3,193
22	111xxx	7	$2,872	0	$0	$2,872
24	111xxx	10	$1,349	0	$0	$1,349
27	111xxx	11	$2,239	0	$0	$2,239
29	111xxx	9	$2,675	0	$0	$2,675
31	111xxx	11	$1,302	0	$0	$1,302
31	111xxx	14	$2,645	0	$0	$2,645
Total		**202**	**$43,700**	**0**	**$0**	**$43,700**

Fixed-Rate Pricing Statement (page 4)

How to read Table 5.4

Day: day of the month that the batch settlement occurred

Ref #: a reference number assigned to each batch settlement for internal and external reporting purposes

 # Sales: number of transactions that were included in the batch settlement

$ Sales: dollar amount of transactions that were included in the batch settlement

 # Credit: number of credits that were included in the batch settlement

$ Credit: dollar amount of credits that were included in the batch settlement

Net Deposit: total amount for each day that was deposited into the merchant's bank account ($ Sales – $ Credit)

Fixed-Rate Pricing Statement (page 5)

Other Fees:

Table 5.5: Fixed-Rate Pricing Statement Other Fees

Number	Amount	Description	Total Fee
26	$6,053.70	Visa Rewards 1	$36.93
1	$85.00	Visa VSP RTL	$0.91
1	$112.50	MC Cross border	$0.45
68	$18,743.50	MC NABU Fee	$1.26
101	$19,353.40	Visa NAPF	$1.97
1	$112.50	MC Foreign Std	$1.59
3	$798.00	Visa EIRF	$10.05
1	$113.00	MC COM Face/Face	$1.46
1	$150.00	MC ENH Merit I	$0.80
22	$7,877.85	MC ENH Merit III	$51.20
1	$104.00	MC WRD ELT Merit 3	$1.16
1	$100.00	Visa CNP	$0.81
1	$350.00	MC World Merit I	$3.50
8	$2,979.00	MC World Merit III	$19.37
1	$300.00	Visa Bus Elect	$4.20
32		Debit Authorization @ $0.10	$3.20
170		Watts Authorization @ $0.10	17.00
21		Batch Header @ $0.25	$5.25
1		Statement @ $10	$10.00
1		PCI Non Compliance @ $19.95	$19.95
		Other Fees Due	$191.06

Fixed-Rate Pricing Statement (page 6)

How to read Table 5.5

This is where the downgrades are applied to specific transactions.

Number: number of transactions for the applicable interchange category or fee category

Amount: dollar amount of transactions for the applicable interchange category or fee category

Description: interchange category or fee category

Total Fee: total "other fees" for the applicable interchange category or fee category

Table 5.6 will provide more information about the columns in Table 5.5.

- Downgrade percentage in Table 5.6 is equal to Total Fee/ Amount ($).
- The all-in rate is equal to the fixed rate of 1.83 percent plus the applicable downgrade percentage.

So much for the nice **low fixed rate** of 1.83 percent that the merchant was promised.

Fixed-Rate Pricing Statement (page 7)

Table 5.6: Fixed-Rate Pricing Statement All-in Rates

Number	Amount ($)	Description	Total Fee	Down-grade %	Explanation
26	$6,053.70	Visa Rewards 1	$36.93	0.61%	All-in rate = 2.44%
1	$85.00	Visa VSP RTL	$0.91	1.07%	All-in rate = 2.90%
1	$112.50	MC Cross border	$0.45		Interchange fee cross-border transactions (0.40%)
68	$18,743.50	MC NABU Fee	$1.26		MasterCard network fee ($0.0185)
101	$19,353.40	Visa NAPF	$1.97		Visa network fee ($0.0195)
1	$112.50	MC Foreign Std	$1.59	1.41%	All-in rate = 3.24%
3	$798.00	Visa EIRF	$10.05	1.26%	All-in rate = 3.09%
1	$113.00	MC COM Face/Face	$1.46	1.29%	All-in rate = 3.12%
1	$150.00	MC ENH Merit I	$0.80	0.53%	All-in rate = 2.36%
22	$7,877.85	MC ENH Merit III	$51.20	0.65%	All-in rate = 2.48%
1	$104.00	MC WRD ELT Merit 3	$1.16	1.12%	All-in rate = 2.95%
1	$100.00	Visa CNP	$0.81	0.81%	All-in rate = 2.64%
1	$350.00	MC World Merit I	$3.50	1.00%	All-in rate = 2.83%
8	$2,979.00	MC World Merit III	$19.37	0.65%	All-in rate = 2.48%
1	$300.00	Visa Bus Elect	$4.20	1.40%	All-in rate = 3.23%
32		Debit Authorization @ $0.10	$3.20		32 debit transactions were assessed at $0.10

Fixed-Rate Pricing Statement (page 8)

Table 5.6: Fixed-Rate Pricing Statement All-in Rates (*continued*)

Number	Amount ($)	Description	Total Fee	Downgrade %	Explanation
170		Watts Authorization @ $0.10	$17.00		170 credit transactions were assessed at $0.10
21		Batch Header @ $0.25	$5.25		21 batch settlements were processed at $0.25 each
1		Monthly Statement @ $10	$10.00		Monthly statement fee
1		PCI Noncompliance @ $19.95	$19.95		Merchant is not PCI compliant
		Total Other Fees Due	$191.06		

Total Fees:

Discount due from Table 5.3	$746.35
Other fees due from Table 5.5	$191.06
Total amount deducted	$937.41

The *blended rate* for this merchant is 2.15 percent ($937.41/$43,700).

This will not be disclosed on your monthly statement.

Three-Tier Pricing Statement (page 1)

Name of MSP

Address

Processing month: xx/xx

Merchant number: xxxxxxxxxxx

Merchant name

Address

Transaction Summary:

Table 5.7: Three-Tier Pricing Statement Transaction Summary

Card Type	# Sales	$ Sales	# Credit	$ Credit	Net Sales	Discount Paid	Per Item Paid
Visa	101	$19,353	0	$0	$19,353	$374.64	$10.10
MasterCard	69	$18,856	0	$0	$18,856	$407.99	$6.90
Discover	0	$0	0	$0	$0	$0	$0
Debit	32	$5,491	0	$0	$5,491	$82.37	$3.20
Total	**202**	**$43,700**	**0**	**$0**	**$43,700**	**$865.00**	**$20.20**

How to read Table 5.7

Card Type: type of credit or debit cards the customers used to make payments in the reporting month

 # Sales: number of sales for each card type in the reporting month

Three-Tier Pricing Statement (page 2)

$ Sales: dollar value of sales for each card type in the reporting month

 # Credit: number of credits for each card type in the reporting month

$ Credit: dollar value of credits for each card type in the reporting month

Net Sales: dollar value of sales minus dollar value of credits for each card type in the reporting month

Discount Paid: total amount of discount rate fees (percentage) paid for each card type in the reporting month (Table 5.9)

Per Item Paid: total amount of transaction fees paid for each card type in the reporting month (Table 5.10)

Three-Tier Pricing Statement (page 3)

Batch Information:

Table 5.8: Three-Tier Pricing Statement Batch Summary

Day	Ref #	# Sales	$ Sales	# Credit	$ Credit	Net Deposit
01	111xxx	4	$430	0	$0	$430
03	111xxx	8	$977	0	$0	$977
03	111xxx	12	$2,141	0	$0	$2,141
05	111xxx	16	$3,523	0	$0	$3,523
06	111xxx	10	$2,604	0	$0	$2,604
06	111xxx	8	$1,031	0	$0	$1,031
08	111xxx	14	$2,784	0	$0	$2,784
10	111xxx	8	$2,883	0	$0	$2,883
12	111xxx	6	$1,773	0	$0	$1,773
13	111xxx	12	$3,049	0	$0	$3,049
15	111xxx	7	$1,369	0	$0	$1,369
17	111xxx	9	$1,357	0	$0	$1,357
17	111xxx	5	$703	0	$0	$703
19	111xxx	10	$2,801	0	$0	$2,801
20	111xxx	11	$3,193	0	$0	$3,193
22	111xxx	7	$2,872	0	$0	$2,872
24	111xxx	10	$1,349	0	$0	$1,349
27	111xxx	11	$2,239	0	$0	$2,239
29	111xxx	9	$2,675	0	$0	$2,675
31	111xxx	11	$1,302	0	$0	$1,302
31	111xxx	14	$2,645	0	$0	$2,645
Totals		**202**	**$43,700**	**0**	**$0**	**$43,700**

How to read Table 5.8

Day: day of the month that the batch settlement occurred

Three-Tier Pricing Statement (page 4)

Ref #: a reference number assigned to each batch settlement for internal and external reporting purposes

 # Sales: number of transactions that were included in the batch settlement

$ Sales: dollar amount of transactions that were included in the batch settlement

 # Credit: number of credits that were included in the batch settlement

$ Credit: dollar amount of credits that were included in the batch settlement

Net Deposit: total amount for each day that was deposited into the merchant's bank account ($ Sales − $ Credit)

Three-Tier Pricing Statement (page 5)

Visa/MC Processing Charges:

Table 5.9: Three-Tier Pricing Statement Discount Rate

Description	Sales Amount	Discount Rate	Total Charges
Visa Qual.	$12,016.30	1.50%	$180.24
Visa Mid-qual.	$6,238.70	2.50%	$155.97
Visa Nonqual.	$1,098.00	3.50%	$38.43
MC Qual.	$7,169.65	1.50%	$107.54
MC Mid-qual.	$10,856.85	2.50%	$271.42
MC Nonqual.	$829.50	3.50%	$29.03
Debit	$5,491.00	1.50%	$82.37
Total	$43,700.00		$865.00

How to read Table 5.9

Description: the tiers that the MSP grouped all of the merchant transactions into (Remember, there are over three hundred interchange categories for Visa, MasterCard, and Discover.)

Sales Amount: aggregate dollar value of sales for each tier

Discount Rate: tier rate that will be applied to each transaction that falls into the applicable tier (This rate is set by the MSP.)

Total Charges: sales amount multiplied by discount rate

Remember, the merchant will never know the exact types of credit and debit cards customers used for their purchases with this type of pricing structure.

Three-Tier Pricing Statement (page 6)

Authorization Fees:

Table 5.10: Three-Tier Pricing Statement Authorization Fees

Description	Items	Transaction Fee	Fee Amount
Visa Watts	101	$0.10	$10.10
MC Watts	69	$0.10	$6.90
Debit	32	$0.10	$3.20
Total	**202**		**$20.20**

How to read Table 5.10

The transaction fee is applied to all authorization attempts.

This merchant is paying $0.10 for each authorization attempt.

Other Fees:

Table 5.11: Three-Tier Pricing Statement Other Fees

Description	Items	Fee Per Item	Fee Amount
Batch Header Fee	21	$0.25	$5.25
Statement	1	$10.00	$10.00
PCI Noncompliance	1	$19.95	$19.95
Total Other Fees	**202**		**$35.20**

Three-Tier Pricing Statement (page 7)

Total Fees:

Visa/MC processing charges from Table 5.9	$865.00
Authorization fees from Table 5.10	$ 20.20
Other fees from Table 5.11	$ 35.20
Total amount deducted	$920.40

The *blended rate* for this merchant is 2.11 percent ($920.40/$43,700).

This will not be disclosed on your monthly statement.

Interchange or Cost-Plus Pricing Statement (page 1)

Name of MSP

Address

Processing month: xx/xx

Merchant number: xxxxxxxxxxx

Merchant name

Address

Transaction Summary:

Table 5.12: Interchange or Cost-Plus Pricing Statement Transaction Summary

Card Type	# Sales	$ Sales	# Credit	$ Credit	Net Sales
Visa	101	$19,353	0	$0	$19,353
MasterCard	69	$18,856	0	$0	$18,856
Discover	0	$0	0	$0	$0
Debit	32	$5,491	0	$0	$5,491
Total	202	$43,700	0	$0	$43,700

Interchange or Cost-Plus Pricing Statement (page 2)

How to read Table 5.12

Card Type: type of credit or debit cards the customers used to make payments in the reporting month

 # Sales: number of sales for each card type in the reporting month

$ Sales: dollar value of sales for each card type in the reporting month

 # Credit: number of credits for each card type in the reporting month

$ Credit: dollar value of credits for each card type in the reporting month

Net Sales: dollar value of sales minus dollar value of credits for each card type in the reporting month

Interchange or Cost-Plus Pricing Statement (page 3)

Batch Information:

Table 5.13: Interchange or Cost-Plus Pricing Statement Batch Summary

Day	Ref#	# Sales	$ Sales	# Credit	$ Credit	Net Deposit
01	111xxx	4	$430	0	$0	$430
03	111xxx	8	$977	0	$0	$977
03	111xxx	12	$2,141	0	$0	$2,141
05	111xxx	16	$3,523	0	$0	$3,523
06	111xxx	10	$2,604	0	$0	$2,604
06	111xxx	8	$1,031	0	$0	$1,031
08	111xxx	14	$2,784	0	$0	$2,784
10	111xxx	8	$2,883	0	$0	$2,883
12	111xxx	6	$1,773	0	$0	$1,773
13	111xxx	12	$3,049	0	$0	$3,049
15	111xxx	7	$1,369	0	$0	$1,369
17	111xxx	9	$1,357	0	$0	$1,357
17	111xxx	5	$703	0	$0	$703
19	111xxx	10	$2,801	0	$0	$2,801
20	111xxx	11	$3,193	0	$0	$3,193
22	111xxx	7	$2,872	0	$0	$2,872
24	111xxx	10	$1,349	0	$0	$1,349
27	111xxx	11	$2,239	0	$0	$2,239
29	111xxx	9	$2,675	0	$0	$2,675
31	111xxx	11	$1,302	0	$0	$1,302
31	111xxx	14	$2,645	0	$0	$2,645
Totals		**202**	**$43,700**	**0**	**$0**	**$43,700**

Interchange or Cost-Plus Pricing Statement (page 4)

How to read Table 5.13

Day: day of the month that the batch settlement occurred

Ref #: a reference number assigned to each batch settlement for internal and external reporting purposes

 # Sales: number of transactions that were included in the batch settlement

$ Sales: dollar amount of transactions that were included in the batch settlement

 # Credit: number of credits that were included in the batch settlement

$ Credit: dollar amount of credits that were included in the batch settlement

Net Deposit: total amount for each day that was deposited into the merchant's bank account ($ Sales − $ Credit)

Interchange or Cost-Plus Pricing Statement (page 5)

Summary of Interchange Fees:

Table 5.14: Interchange or Cost-Plus Pricing Statement Interchange Fees

Interchange Category	Discount Rate	Per Item	Count	Volume	Total Fee
Visa—Non-Debit					
Rewards 1	1.65%	$0.10	26	$6,053.70	$102.49
VSP Retail	1.54%	$0.10	1	$85.00	$1.41
EIRF	2.30%	$0.10	3	$798.00	$18.65
CNP	1.80%	$0.10	1	$100.00	$1.90
Business Elect	2.40%	$0.10	1	$300.00	$7.30
Retail Credit	1.54%	$0.10	69	$12,016.30	$191.95
Total Visa—Non-Debit			101	$19,353.00	$323.70
MasterCard—Non-Debit					
Foreign Standard	2.15%	$0.10	1	$112.50	$2.52
Comm Face to Face	2.15%	$0.10	1	$113.00	$2.53
Enhanced Merit I	2.04%	$0.10	1	$150.00	$3.16
Enhanced Merit III	1.73%	$0.10	22	$7,877.85	$138.49
World Elite Merit III	2.20%	$0.10	1	$104.00	$2.39
World Merit I	2.08%	$0.10	1	$350.00	$7.38
World Merit III	1.73%	$0.10	8	$2,979.00	$52.34
Retail Credit	1.58%	$0.10	34	7,169.65	$116.68
Total MasterCard—Non-Debit			69	$18,856.00	$325.49

Interchange or Cost-Plus Pricing Statement (page 6)

Table 5.14: Interchange or Cost-Plus Pricing Statement Interchange
Fees (*continued*)

Interchange Category	Discount Rate	Per Item	Count	Volume	Total Fee
Regulated Debit					
MasterCard and Visa	0.05%	$0.21	32	$5,491	$9.47
Total Interchange			202	$43,700.00	$658.66

How to read Table 5.14

Interchange Category: the specific interchange category the
transactions qualified for based on Visa and MasterCard's criteria

Discount Rate: the portion of the interchange fee, expressed as a
percentage, for the applicable interchange category (The discount rate
is multiplied by the volume to determine the actual dollar amount
of the fee.)

Per Item: the portion of the interchange fee, expressed on a per
transaction or "per swipe" basis, for the applicable interchange
category (The per-item amount or transaction fee is multiplied by
the count to determine the actual dollar amount of the fee.)

Count: number of sales in each interchange category for the reporting
month

Volume: aggregate dollar amount of sales in each interchange
category for the reporting month

Total Fee: total interchange fee for each interchange category
(Calculated as [discount rate × volume] + [per item × count].)

Interchange or Cost-Plus Pricing Statement (page 7)

Summary of Card Fees:

Table 5.15: Interchange or Cost-Plus Pricing Statement Card Fees

Card Fee Description	# Sales	$ Sales	Rate (%)/Per Item ($)	Card Fee Amount
Visa Credit				
Discount		$19,353.00	0.20%	$38.71
Auth	101		$0.10	$10.10
Assessment		$19,353.00	0.11%	$21.29
NAPF	101		$0.0195	$1.97
Total Visa Credit				**$72.07**
MasterCard Credit				
Discount		$18,856.00	0.20%	$37.71
Auth	69		$0.10	$6.90
Assessment		$18,856.00	0.11%	$20.74
NABU	69		$0.0185	$1.28
Cross Border		$112.50	0.40%	$0.45
Total MasterCard Credit				**$67.08**

Interchange or Cost-Plus Pricing Statement (page 8)

Table 5.15: Interchange or Cost-Plus Pricing Statement Card Fees (*continued*)

Card Fee Description	# Sales	$ Sales	Rate (%)/Per Item ($)	Card Fee Amount
Debit				
Discount		$5,491.00	0.20%	$10.98
Auth	32		$0.10	$3.20
Assessment		$5,491.00	0.11%	$6.04
Network (assumed all Visa)	32		$0.0195	$0.62
Total Debit				**$20.84**
Total Card Fees				**$159.99**
Other Fees				
Statement Fee			$10.00	$10.00
PCI Noncompliance			$19.95	$19.95
Total Other Fees			$29.95	**$29.95**

How to read Table 5.15

With interchange or cost-plus pricing, this section is where you will find out exactly what you are paying above and beyond the interchange fees.

Interchange or Cost-Plus Pricing Statement (page 9)

Discount: the discount rate that is multiplied by the $ Sales (This fee goes to the MSP.)

Auth: the transaction fee that is multiplied by the # Sales (This fee goes to the MSP.)

Assessment: fees to Visa/MasterCard

NAPF and NABU: network fee that goes to Visa/MasterCard

Cross Border: a portion of the interchange fee that is charged if the card used by the customer was issued by a foreign bank

 # Sales: number of transactions in the reporting month

$ Sales: aggregate dollar amount of transactions in the reporting month

Rate (%)/Per Item ($): applicable percentage or per item fee

Card Fee Amount: either [# Sales × Per Item ($)] or [$ Sales × Rate (%)]

Total Fees:

Total interchange fees from Table 5.14	$658.66
Total card fees from Table 5.15	$159.99
Total other fees from Table 5.15	$ 29.95
Total amount deducted	$848.60

The *blended rate* for this merchant is 1.94 percent ($848.60/$43,700).

This will not be disclosed on your monthly statement.

Summary Information

Table 5.16: The Right Pricing Strategy for Your Business

Cost to Merchant with Fixed-Rate Pricing (1.83 percent fixed rate)	Cost to Merchant with Three-Tier Pricing	Cost to Merchant with Interchange or Cost-Plus Pricing (20 bps/$0.10)
(A)	(B)	(C)
$937.41 or a 2.15 percent blended all-in rate	$920.40 or a 2.11 percent blended all-in rate	$848.60 or a 1.94 percent all-in rate

Which would you rather pay?

CHAPTER 6
PCI Compliance:
Why Do You Care?

This chapter will discuss

- PCI definition and details;
- PCI objectives and requirements; and
- additional PCI resources.

Every consumer wants to know their credit and debit card account information is secure. Offering your customers a safe and secure payment method is no longer just good business practice; it is a *requirement of doing business.*

As a business accepting credit and debit cards for payment for goods or services, you are responsible for safeguarding cardholder information, and ultimately you can be held liable for any breaches in security. Fines for noncompliance can cost a business thousands of dollars or more.

The *Payment Card Industry Data Security Standard* (PCI DSS) is a worldwide information security standard assembled by the founding payment brands of the Payment Card Industry Security Standards Council (PCI SSC), including American Express, Discover Financial Services, JCB International, MasterCard Worldwide, and Visa Inc. International. The PCI DSS is a set of comprehensive requirements designed to help organizations proactively protect customer account data.

Does this apply to every business?

PCI compliance mandates apply to all organizations that store, transmit, or process cardholder data (Visa, MasterCard, Discover, and American Express) regardless of how they accept payments from their customers (in person, online, via mail order, or telephone order). The degree of proof of compliance will be determined by an organizations merchant level.

What are the requirements of PCI DSS?

There are six objectives and twelve requirements, which are categorized in Table 6.1. The PCI Security Standards website (www. pcisecuritystandards.org) refers to this information as "PCI Data Security Standard—High Level Overview."

Table 6.1: PCI Objectives and Requirements

Objective	Requirements
Build and maintain a secure network	01. Install and maintain a firewall configuration to protect cardholder data
	02. Do not use vendor-supplied defaults for system passwords and other security parameters
Protect cardholder data	03. Protect stored cardholder data
	04. Encrypt transmission of cardholder data across open public networks

Table 6.1: PCI Objectives and Requirements (*continued*)

Objective	Requirements
Maintain a vulnerability management program	05. Use and regularly update antivirus software programs 06. Develop and maintain secure systems and applications
Implement strong access control measures	07. Restrict access to cardholder data by business need-to-know 08. Assign a unique ID to each person with computer access 09. Restrict physical access to cardholder data
Regularly monitor and test networks	10. Track and monitor all access to network resources and cardholder data 11. Regularly test security systems and processes
Maintain an information security policy	12. Maintain a policy that addresses information security for all personnel

Validation of Compliance

The mandate to comply with the PCI DSS requires each merchant to verify and demonstrate its compliance status on an annual basis. Validation of compliance identifies and corrects vulnerabilities and further protects customers by ensuring that appropriate levels of cardholder information security are maintained.

Merchant Levels of Compliance

Merchant validation levels vary by processing volume, and it's important for you to know what actions you need to take to validate your compliance. Visa and MasterCard have both imposed severe fines on merchants who are found to be PCI DSS noncompliant at the time of a data breach concerning cardholder information. Avoiding these severe fines is easy to do.

Becoming PCI compliant is not as difficult as many merchants might think. If you are a small to midsize business accepting face-to-face transactions using a standalone credit card terminal, you will likely fall into the lowest level of requirements and have to answer a self-assessment questionnaire. In addition, if your credit card terminal or POS connection is through an IP (Internet) line, the third party PCI provider will also need to do a network scan of the IP address. This entire process should take a merchant no longer than two hours and once completed will ensure they are PCI compliant with appropriate certification.

If a merchant is not PCI compliant, the MSP will, in all likelihood, charge the merchant a PCI noncompliance fee, which can range from $19.99 to $29.99 a month.

As a business owner, you owe it to your clients to make sure you are PCI compliant. Take the time, do it right, and avoid unnecessary additional monthly fees.

Additional PCI Resources:

www.pcisecuritystandards.org

usa.visa.com/merchants/risk_management/cisp.html

www.mastercard.com/us/merchant/support/merchant_education
.html

CHAPTER 7
The Durbin Amendment: What Does It Mean to You?

This chapter will discuss

- basic Durbin Amendment information; and
- Durbin Amendment impact on merchants.

On October 1, 2011, new rules went into effect that lowered the debit card interchange fees that Visa, MasterCard, and Discover charge as the pure cost to process certain types of debit cards.

These changes resulting from the *Durbin Amendment*, passed last year as part of the *Dodd–Frank Wall Street Reform and Consumer Protection Act*, have met with considerable controversy and debate.

Credit and debit card processing costs are often a merchant's second-highest expense after labor, so lower swipe fees for debit cards should be a welcome development, particularly as debit cards have grown in popularity with consumers, surpassing both checks and credit cards. Debit card transactions in the United States totaled close to $25 billion in 2006, and by 2009 the number had reached around $40 billion.

Issuing banks stand to lose billions of dollars by this reduction in debit interchange fees, and merchants are hopeful that these lower costs will be passed through to them, resulting in a financial benefit to the merchant and their customers.

To make up for the anticipated loss in revenue from the lower swipe fees, many issuing banks have begun tacking on new checking account fees and raising minimum balance requirements, and some have threatened to cap the dollar amount for debit transactions and end debit card rewards programs. At the same time, banks are trying to renew customer interest in more profitable credit cards and prepaid debit cards with offers of low interest and rewards bonuses.

Prior to the implementation of the Durbin Amendment, the total interchange fee for an average debit card transaction (approximately $50) was *$0.44 per transaction.* Under the Durbin Amendment, the Federal Reserve has set a cap of *$0.21 per transaction,* which means that it costs the acquiring bank on average *$0.23 less* to conduct that same debit card transaction. For certain acquiring banks, the cap will be $0.22 per transaction if the issuing bank has met certain fraud prevention levels.

It is important to note that the new rules apply only to Visa, MasterCard, and Discover debit cards and *not* credit cards and only to issuing banks with more than $10 billion in assets.

So, what's the bottom line for merchants?

It depends on one simple thing. How is your merchant account priced?

- If you are on a fixed-rate or three-tier pricing program, in all likelihood, the reduced cost to process a debit card will go right into the MSP's pocket. In fact there are many merchant services providers that have used this change to debit card interchange fees as a reason to increase their clients' overall fee structure.

- If you are on interchange or cost-plus pricing, these savings will be directly passed through to your business because all interchange fees—and now these reduced costs—will be passed through.

Merchants that accept a large amount of debit cards and have an average ticket of twenty dollars or more should see a significant cost reduction as a result of the new debit card interchange fees.

Remember, you will only see this benefit if you are priced on an interchange or cost-plus pricing strategy.

CHAPTER 8
A Checklist to Use Before You Make a Decision

This chapter will discuss

- a must-read checklist for all business owners.

1. Will the merchant agreement you have to sign contain an early termination fee?

Read the fine print so you know exactly what you are signing. What is your contract term, and what will it cost you to terminate the agreement if you decide to make a change prior to the end of the contract term?

2. Is there a monthly or annual minimum required?

It is your right as a merchant to only pay for the transactions that you process. If the merchant services provider you are speaking with has monthly or annual fee minimums, then you should probably look elsewhere. There are plenty of merchant services providers out there that do not have this requirement.

3. Were you asked if you want to lease a terminal?

Leasing credit card equipment is one of the biggest moneymakers for MSPs. A fee of $39.99 a month might sound like a small amount to have a brand-new terminal in your store, but if you are paying that for thirty-six months, then you are paying $1,440 in total lease payments ($39.99 × 36 months).

In all likelihood, you can buy a perfectly good credit card terminal for under $400. Which would you rather pay—$1,440 or $400?

High-quality merchant services providers will stand by the technology products they sell to clients; this should include providing loaner machines and expediting any repairs that need to be made.

4. Are you being offered a free credit card terminal?

Remember, nothing in life is free. Either the cost of the credit card terminal will be made up in your monthly processing fees and/or if you do a high volume of transactions, the MSP will only allow you to use that credit card terminal as long as you maintain a merchant account with them. If you cancel the merchant account, the credit card terminal will be taken away.

5. Are you being offered the option of interchange or cost-plus pricing for your merchant account?

Hopefully by now it is 100 percent clear that interchange or cost-plus pricing is the best pricing strategy for any merchant. Nothing else needs to be said.

6. Are you being offered one "super-low" rate for all transactions?

Hopefully by now you know to avoid these types of sales tactics. There is no such thing as one low rate in merchant services. Ask about downgrades, and challenge the salesperson to be straight up with you. The more you know, the more you can save.

7. Will you have 24/7 live support?

All merchant services providers have a support group. What every merchant wants is support that will be there when they need it and a live person to speak with. Most of the time a merchant's questions can easily be answered over the phone, but if you have to wait to speak to someone you are most likely losing business.

8. Ask for referrals.

If you are at all concerned about a specific company that approaches you about your merchant account, ask to speak to some of their existing customers. If they do not readily provide that information to you, you probably need to keep looking.

9. Who is the actual acquiring bank/processor behind the scenes making sure the transactions are moving properly?

It is always important to know who you will be executing your agreement with. There are a lot of acquirers/processors in the market. You need to be sure that you team up with the right organizations.

CHAPTER 9
American Express

Virtually all merchants are aware of American Express and their roughly 25 percent market share in overall credit/debit card volume. Unlike Visa and MasterCard, which are bank associations, American Express is a financial organization that issues credit cards and acquires transactions.

Merchants can either use their merchant services provider to process American Express transactions or can connect directly with American Express. When a merchant services provider is utilized, there is typically an additional transaction fee associated with each authorization request that is paid to the MSP, in addition to the fees charged by American Express. For large commercial clients with significant transaction volume and a direct communication connection with American Express, there is typically no additional transaction fee.

Certain merchants have made the decision to not accept American Express cards from their customers because their understanding is that the fees they will pay to American Express are significantly higher than what they pay on Visa and MasterCard transactions. The fact is that it depends on the type of business and the volume of business that would be going to American Express that determines the discount rate. In certain cases, American Express can be cheaper for a merchant to accept than they might think.

For small and midsize merchants, American Express has certain cost-effective programs that work directly with the MSP, providing the convenience of a single source for statements, settlement, and customer service for all major card brands. In addition, with certain American Express programs, next-day funding is available to the merchant. Asking the right questions and having a good working relationship with your MSP sales person is the key to understanding all of the various options that American Express has to offer.

If you do not currently accept American Express, it is worth a conversation with your merchant services provider to fully understand what options are available and what your American Express rate would be.

It might be lower than you would expect.

Epilogue

I am confident that after reading all of the chapters, you now have a much clearer understanding of the merchant services industry and how you, as a business owner, can negotiate a better contract for your organization.

Remember, a good merchant services provider will walk you through all of the information that has been presented in this book. An MSP that is not willing to do that is not the right organization to work with.

I will leave you with one final thought.

I have been asked hundreds of times by clients and potential clients the following question:

"Why hasn't anyone ever told me this information before?"

The simple answer is this:

"The less you know, the more the merchant services provider can make."

Be in the know.

Take control of your internal costs.

Negotiate the best possible deal for your company.

If you need assistance, I am always available to help:

mmintz@mcmsalesconsulting.com

Index

A

ABA (American Banking Association), 1

ABA routing number, 1

ACH (automated clearing house), 1, 3

acquiring bank (acquirer), 2, 15, 19–20, 32–33, 95

additional fees, 6, 51–55

adjustment, 2

all-in rate, 41–43, 50, 66, 85

American Express

    about, 96–97

    card verification code (CID), 5

    defined, 2

    and PCI compliance, 86-87

AMG Payment Solutions, 15

annual fee minimums, 93

annual fees, 2, 53, 93

application fee, 2

approval, 2, 15, 18, 20, 51

ARU (automated response unit), 13

assessment fees, 3, 7, 26–27, 30–31, 38, 49-50, 59, 82–84

authorization, 3, 12

authorization code, 3

authorization fees, 26–28, 51, 74

automatic bill payment, 3

average ticket (average transaction amount), 4

AVS (address verification service), 2, 27

B

B2B electronic solutions, 14

banks, role in transactions, 35–36

basis point, 4, 31, 34, 45, 49, 60

batch, 4, 63, 71, 78

batch header fees, 52, 65, 68, 74

batch settlement, 4, 19, 52, 57

batch settlement fees, 59–60

Boost Payment Solutions, 14

business cards, 5, 13–14, 46–47

buy rates, 15, 33–36

C

capture, 4, 12–13

card associations, 4, 30-31. *See also specific associations*

card-present transactions, 5, 11, 23–25

chargeback, 5, 11

chargeback fee, 54–55

CNP (card-not-present) transactions, 2, 5, 7–8, 23–25, 38

commercial cards, 5

corporate cards, 5, 9, 23

credit, defined, 5

credit card terminals, 8, 12-13, 17, 19, 89, 93–94

credit cards

    interchange fees, 25

    ways merchants accept, 12-13

customer service fee, 53

V

W